HOW TO ACQUIRE
GREAT LEADERSHIP ABILITIES
IN THE ABSENCE OF FEAR

BASED ON THE BOOK OF EXODUS

PASTOR REGINA C. BRENT

CLAY BRIDGES
PRESS

**How To Acquire Great Leadership Abilities
In The Absence Of Fear**
Copyright © 2017 by Pastor Regina C. Brent

Publication made possible through
Extended Hands of Jesus Ministry.

ISBN 10: 1939815290

ISBN 13: 9781939815293

eISBN 10: 1939815304

eISBN 13: 9781939815309

TABLE OF CONTENTS

*This book is dedicated to the Precious Holy Spirit
and the Body of Christ.*

FOREWORD

Why did God give Moses a deliverance ministry? For the same reason He is calling the church into this same ministry today. The answer to this question can be found in Exodus 3:8-9. First, God wanted Moses to deliver his people out of the hands of their oppressors so that he could take them to a land flowing with milk and honey. Secondly, so that God's people would worship the Lord their God in the environment of praise and worship on His Mountain. (Exodus 3:12). Worship leads us closer to God's presence. God gave them favor so they did not leave Egypt empty handed. (Ex. 3:21-22). A service called forth by God for each and every one of us. Will you be that man or woman who would humble yourself before God and say, "Here I am Lord, use me?" Jesus said He came to set the captives free. We are His handiwork and laborers together with Him.

Let this be our prayer:

Let thy Spirit rise up within me Oh Lord.

Let the living waters flow that I may grow.

Humble me and set thy task upon me.

Let thy Spirit take lead that I might set your
people free.

Cast out all anxiety and fear.

Let it not dwell in this temple here.

Set my feet on the path of your Word.

Let me live on what I have heard.

Through Your Son Jesus Christ I pray. AMEN.

INTRODUCTION

Before God created man, the Spirit hovered over the waters in Gen. 1:2. So was Moses drawn from the waters as a baby to be blessed by the wealth and knowledge of Egypt. Water refreshes us, quenches our thirst, and cleanses us. Water is a symbol of the Holy Spirit. Man needs water in order to survive. Jesus calls those who are thirsty. He is the Fountain of life that helps us to survive and whoever believes in Him, He said out of his heart living waters will flow. (John 7:37-39). Verse 39 explains that Jesus was referring to the Spirit whom those believing in Him would receive. The human body is made up mostly of water and I have known many people, including my sister, who ended up in the hospital because of dehydration. Water preserves the life of man the same way the Word of God and His life giving Spirit preserves us. We must never suffer from spiritual dehydration by neglecting to fill our heart and soul with the water of word of God.

We all know the story of how Moses came to the mountain of God in Midian and the Angel of the Lord appeared to him out of a burning bush. (Ex. 3:1-2). Moses sought the Lord upon the mountain and found Him. He became a little reluctant, but listened to the voice of the Lord, obeyed, and followed God's instruction. God gave him a shepherd's staff. A shepherd's staff in the hand is a symbol of preparation for service.

God then gave Moses the task of delivering his people from bondage and assured him that He would be with him. (Ex. 3:12). As a result, Moses became an instrument in the hands of God preparing the way for deliverance of God's people from heavy bondage. Moses' name means "drawn out".

The people of Israel cried out to the Lord in prayer to deliver them from heavy bondage so God gave His people a "Deliverer", a man called "Moses" to draw them out from their affliction.

The Lord told me a while back that this is the way He births ministries in the earth. He hears the cries of His people, then chooses someone after His own heart to accomplish this task on earth. Someone who says, "Here I am Lord, use me."

The ministry of deliverance calls for an individual that is endowed with the Spirit of God and with all the fruit of the Spirit: Love, joy, peace, gentleness, kindness, patience, goodness, and self-control. (Gal. 5:22). Anyone who desires to lead must first know how to follow. They must know how to submit and commit themselves to follow the will of the Lord in all matters of the heart.

Not everyone is patient, kind, and peace loving. God is our Help and although leaders carry such a heavy crown, God is able to lighten it and labor together with them hand in hand. Be encouraged. God orders our steps and if we just open up our heart to Him, He will take the lead.

WE FACE FEAR EVERYDAY EVEN THOUGH WE ARE NOT KEENLY AWARE OF IT. I PRAY THAT IN THE READING OF THIS BOOK, YOU WILL BE SAVED AND DELIVERED FROM THE SPIRIT OF FEAR.

BOOKS OF THE OLD TESTAMENT

I love to study the books of the Old Testament for the following reasons:

1. The Old Testament vividly shows the character of God and how He forms lasting, meaningful covenant relationships. God gives examples not only of what He expects from individuals in one-on-one personal relationships, but also of how He interacts with peoples and nations.

2. The Old Testament records how God used prophets to anoint particular people into ministry. People whose hearts were stirred to do God's will, people who were prepared to receive His spirit to accomplish a particular task He had chosen for them.

3. The Old Testament shows how God delivered His people and how He accomplished it either

by sending forth angels, by His own hand, or spoke through someone whom He'd chosen.

4. The Old Testament illustrates how God enacted laws and judgments for His people. (See the Books of Leviticus and Deuteronomy).

5. Men in the Old Testament had an active prayer life as we will see from the text.

Before I begin, I would like to state that the best leader in the world is the person who carries the gospel of Jesus Christ to others and ultimately brings them into the kingdom of God. God's heart is for lost souls. (2 Pet. 3:9). Cast your net and become a fisher of men.

It doesn't matter whether you are President of a nation, of a corporation, a pastor of a church, an individual with a particular call to ministry, a father or mother, or just a person with some kind of responsibility; we have all experienced some kind of fear.

LEADERSHIP: DEPENDING ON GOD

Are you someone who is seeking a leadership position, or just a person who is responsible for his own well being? I pray that the wisdom I received from God on the subject of fear will bless your life tremendously. Fear touches everyone's life in one way or another (i.e. terminal illness, phobias, terrorism, a sudden loss [death] of a loved one, change in employment, moving to another city, etc.).

Fear, if not restrained, can be destructive. Let us read the gospel of Mark, Chapter 11, verses 15-18 ["The Moneychangers"].

Why were the chief priests and scribes so afraid of Jesus that they sought to destroy Him? People were more attentive to the teaching of Jesus Christ. Truth holds up a transparent mirror that opens the gateway to self. It is very hard for most people to

How To Acquire Great Leadership Abilities
In The Absence Of Fear

accept truth, especially when it involves a personal correction or chastisement. In reading this word, fear can bring about a spirit of destruction. We fear when we lose control of a situation.

Psalm 56:3 – When we are afraid, God is our trust

Prayer coverage either by oneself, church members, or intercessors can be very helpful and supportive. This writing came about as I was reading the Book of Exodus. The Spirit of the Lord came upon me to reveal this word about the "spirit of fear."

If you are an individual looking for answers, unconditional love, and freedom from fear, God's Word will give you the answer. If you do not know how to find Him, His Word will give you directions. (Prov. 8:17). We must earnestly and continually press on in prayer and love Him with our whole heart. Intimacy with God is the key to overcoming fear. Moses was diligent in pursuing God.

As I chart this course in writing about leadership through the wilderness, you shall see how the sins of lawlessness and rebellion oppose any kind of authority; whether it was in Moses' day or today as events unfold in prophecy.

The Lord told me years ago that Moses was the greatest intercessor. His close relationship with the

Lord as a leader and his devotion and obedience to Him helped him to endure opposition and hardship, and gave him the courage to move forward in the midst of trials and adversities.

Bondage can either be physical, spiritual, or both. God used Moses to bring salvation in both incidences. Moses carried the Word of God from the mountain and spoke it to the people of Israel, and led them out of captivity.

THE BELIEVER'S POSITION

We are a chosen race; a royal priesthood; a holy nation; *a people for God's own possession.* (I Peter 2:9).

Leaders carry very heavy responsibilities. They encounter many problems and become very discouraged just like we do. Exodus means "Exit", migration, or pathway out. People today are migrating to other countries and becoming refugees in other lands for reasons of escape from war and oppression. I pray that this information will encourage them and you, bless you, and show you the way out so that you can acquire greater leadership abilities in the absence of fear.

In the book of Exodus, time and time again Moses made intercession for his people as well as his enemies. He had an ongoing, daily, face-to-face communication with God. Again and again, God's hand moved in a mighty way with each of Moses' petitions. To entreat the Lord and call upon Him is a great and wonderful privilege. (Ex. 24:18).

You can be a great leader or a great person and still not have a reverent fear of God. Pharaoh demonstrates this in the book of Exodus. Pharaoh depended on his own power, his army, and his magicians to accomplish his goal. Moses depended on God to accomplish his.

THE PEOPLE OF ISRAEL

God has chosen the people of Israel as a reminder to the world that there is a God in Israel and that He is one with us.

For decades there have been news reports and historical events between Israel and other nations. Millions of Jews were killed by Hitler and placed in concentration camps. Former Presidents of the United States have participated in peace negotiations between Israel and other nations and nations today, like Pharaoh, keep watch over Israel and Jerusalem. The United Nations and the Middle East are very preoccupied with their territory and their future. Their miraculous survival is explained by the presence of a God of Israel Who watches over this land of chosen people and Who has placed His name in Jerusalem. (2 Kings 21:4). Jesus ministered in that part of the world and Christian believers visit the holy sites of Israel and Jerusalem today. The importance of this nation stems from the Book of Isaiah:

Israel:

- God is called the Holy and Mighty One of Israel in Isa. 1:24.
- He is the God of Israel in Isa. 21:10.
- He is the Rock of Israel in Isa. 30;29.
- He is Redeemer of Israel in Isa. 49:7.

Jerusalem:

1. Isa. 4:1-3: In a vision of the coming kingdom (v. 3) – Those who abide in Jerusalem will be called holy. In present day, President Trump is currently considering moving the U.S. Embassy there. Nothing has been decided yet.

2. Isa. 27:13: It is where God's holy mountain is to call His people to worship.

3. Isa. 37:32: The surviving remnant goes forth from there. (2 Kings 19:31).

4. God's promise in Isa. 62:6-7: Jerusalem will be praise in the earth.

FEAR AND BONDAGE

How did the children of Israel end up in bitter bondage for so many years? Let's go back to the book of Exodus, chapter one. As we can see, the *"Spirit of Fear"* was the catalyst. A new king arose in Egypt and beheld the people of Israel. He determined in his heart, through latent fear, that they were a great nation and a mighty people. He was afraid that they would multiply their numbers and eventually turn against the people of Egypt. The king's fear caused him to assign taskmasters to afflict them with hard labor and cruel treatment. (Exodus 1:8-11). And so the lives of innocent people came under the control of a fearful and suspicious king. Through fear of the unknown, a king sought to control the destiny of an entire nation. Fear of the unknown gives way to control.

History has proven that even members of a

royal family as well as a leader's military will turn on them for power and control of the throne. Kim Jong Un, the president of North Korea, had some of his family members killed. He may have had good reasons or bad; no one knows. Here in America, Presidents Abraham Lincoln and John F. Kennedy were assassinated and President Ronald Reagan escaped an assassin's bullet as well. A death threat usually comes with a leader's position of power and is a part of carrying the weight of fear and anxiety. I pray that every leader will have knowledge of God because salvation comes from the Lord and in Him and through Jesus Christ we have eternal life.

Moses was almost killed (Exodus 2:11-15) and he feared for his life after killing an Egyptian. Many presidents, leaders, and prime ministers have had death threats while completing their term in office. This is another aspect of holding such a powerful position. Although some hire protection like the Secret Service or depend upon the military, no one is found to be trustworthy except God our Savior.

In the Body of Christ, pastors fear they won't meet their budget or that they will lose membership. They also have personal problems and health problems just like us. In every case, leaders must find peace with God and make Him the center of their lives. Above all, lift God up higher than yourself and your situations and keep Him in that position. God will keep your position if you will hold fast to HisGod's placement and priority in our lives is more important than our fears. Surrender everything to Him and let Him take control.

God has taught me over the years how destructive the spirit of fear and control can be. In my own life, I have found that in some incidences, a spirit of fear can hinder you from receiving your healing and moving forward in your ministry.

In the spring of 1994, my physician told me that I had a lesion in my breast. Fear came into my spirit, but God spoke to me. He said repeatedly, "Pray it off." Fear can hinder your healing. I prayed and prayed and about two (2) days later, the fear finally left my spirit. Afterwards, I received a miraculous healing. Even the doctors were astounded. Fear can cause irreparable damage to the mind, soul, body, and spirit, as you will see through this writing.

As Shepherd, you present new information about issues and changes in the church body. Remember, we are still humans and fall short of God's glory. Suddenly, either at a church meeting, or in person, one or more members approach you and is in disagreement about the change. They leave the church in anger and without counsel. I have experienced this in a church in which I was a member and the topic of debate was "A Woman's Role in the Church" based upon Galatians 3:28.

There was another issue about speaking in tongues. The staff said they did not have a problem with speaking in tongues as long as there was interpretation. You have to know the word so you can be ready with an answer. This is accurate scripture cited in I Corinthians 14:27-28.

I have had many calls from other churches well known in the Houston area and their members would call me about questions they had concerns about. First, I would ask them if they had a church home or a pastor. If the answer was yes, I would tell them to consult with their own pastor. Their response was, "My pastor is unapproachable." I would then answer their question. We are all one in the Body of Christ. Some members are afraid to speak to their pastors. If the work load is too much to bear, pray to God for the right people to assist you; people after God's own heart. Appoint men and women of integrity and a good moral character. In mega churches, people tend to get lost in the system. Jethro, Moses' father-in-law, gave him the same advice. (Ex. 18:7-23).

Pastors are mostly concerned about their sermons being accepted, light bills, church repairs, new carpeting, a new bell, choir robes, etc. Burdens cannot be controlled but God says His love controls us. Give it over to Him and if we place our petition before His throne of grace and quietly listen, we will find the answer.

FEAR AND CONTROL

Fear can hinder you from obeying the voice of God. The Lord told me that Psalm 127 was for leaders. God must build the house and our ears must be attentive to Him and not ourselves or anyone else. Otherwise, our labor would be in vain. "Control" is very subtle and without even realizing it, we are unexpectedly ensnared by its effect. We need to discern when to let go and let God take control.

Fear comes by way of manipulation and control (money can also be a source of control). Bribes will cause the innocent to suffer and will destroy any remedy of fair justice under the law. Another example is abuse. Many people (unemployed or who have low self esteem) who depend on their spouses to provide for their welfare will not confess any physical abuse to law enforcement officials or anyone else because they fear they will never make it on their own or find anyone else. I have good news, "With God all things are possible!"

Exodus 5:2 – Pharaoh had no knowledge of the Lord so he questioned Moses by asking who this God was that he should obey His command to release His people. Indeed, if he knew the Lord, he would have surely let the people go. God is a God who is feared among the nations. This king not only took control of the situation, but for good measure, threw in pride and arrogance as well. How can we obey the Lord if we will not acknowledge Him or hearken to His voice? The spirit of control places you and other people around you in bondage. Here is the formula: Fear + Control = Bondage.

Repeatedly, the Lord sent Moses back to tell Pharaoh to let His people go so that they might serve Him but Pharaoh did not want to give up control. The spirit of control forces its way intruding on people's minds and lives. Jesus is all about freedom to choose. The spirit of control can hinder people from obeying God and serving Him. How? God gives us free will. He allows us to make our own decisions, our own mistakes. Even Adam and Eve had a choice. Controlling someone's mind (mind control) is witchcraft. A spirit of control can cause a heart to be hardened, as in the case of Pharaoh. God hardens hearts so that He may show signs and wonders. (Rom. 9:17-18). God hardened Pharaoh's heart so that He could reveal Himself to Pharaoh in a more powerful way.

David and King Saul: Saul also feared losing his crown and position as king because God had already chosen David who gained favor with Him and the people favored him after his victory over the Philistines. This fear led to jealousy and attempted murder. Saul tried to kill David on several occasions.

Cain and Abel: In Genesis, the Lord favored Abel's offering and rejected Cain's so Cain, out of anger, killed his brother Abel. People will kill what they can't control. We see this same mindset in terrorists today: Take, take, take by kidnapping other people's children, murder and rape, etc. It is a willful and selfish act. A will of control push people to the breaking point when they are not in agreement; their reasoning is, 'either comply or move out of my way.'

Eventually, the Spirit of God left Saul because of his disobedience and he was empty of truth and Godly counsel. God's Spirit and truth brings light but Saul was in darkness so God gave His lamp to David. Sometimes when the spirit of control fails to have its own way, it resorts to sorcery and witchcraft. A good example of this is found in the book of I Samuel when Saul sought out the witch of Endor because he feared the Philistines. (I Sam. 28:5-9). Today's psychic hot lines are no different. People today are seeking man instead of God. They consult people with dark powers because they fear for their future. When Pharaoh needed counsel, he called forth his magicians. (Ex. 7:11).

Sorcery is the use of power gained from the assistance or control of evil spirits for predicting the future or divining. In the Old Testament, sorcerers were not allowed to live. (Ex. 22:18). Today, through the sacrifice of Jesus Christ, all of our sins have been removed and redemption has come to everyone who would believe on the name of Jesus Christ. Anyone can be saved if they just open up their hearts to Him. We should pray for people who operate in witchcraft and sorcery. Ask Jesus to convict their hearts and pray that He will sanctify them in the truth of His Word.

The Words of Jesus – (Rev. 22:12-15).

We have seen historically and in present day how people want to take control of their own destinies and those of other people. Only God has the power over life and death. Only God is the Wonderful Counselor, mighty in word and deeds. Let go of control and give it to God.

Let's take a look at these two scenarios on Leadership Roles:

Pharaoh (King of Egypt):

Source of Israel's Bondage:	The King's fear.
Action Taken:	Placing people in bitter bondage and seeking magicians to solve his problems.
Reasoning:	To maintain power and control over the destiny of a nation.

Saul (King of Israel):

Source of Downfall:	Disobedience/Fear/Jealousy
Action Taken:	Attempted murder and loss of his kingdom eventually led him to seeking out witches.
Reasoning:	Refusing to hear

God's truth from the prophet; wanting to maintain power and control over his own destiny while at the same time trying to destroy David's.

The end result was tragic for both of these powerful leaders.

I personally believe that Saul's jealousy and selfish ambition came from the fear of losing his family's love and attention to David. His son Jonathan was a close friend to David and his daughter was married to him. There are people who fear their admiration is being stolen from others and have a desperate need for attention. We will always have God's attention and God desires yours as well. He is ever near and not far.

THE SPIRIT OF JEZEBEL

In I Kings 19:1-18, Elijah runs in fear for his life from Jezebel. He prayed that he might die. He told the Lord to take his life. Instead, the Lord gave him rest and nourishment. As Elijah rested, an angel ministered to him by saying, "Arise and eat." Characteristics of the spirit of Jezebel include deception, control, domination, and manipulation. I have personally experienced this spirit operating in my own ministry as well as other churches.

The spirit of control called "Jezebel": Francis Frangipane is one of my favorite Christian writers of this day and time. He wrote a book called, "The Jezebel Spirit." I highly recommend reading it. In chapter two, he said in citing I Kings 19:4, "What pressure overwhelmed this great man of God (the prophet Elijah) that he would fall prey to fear and discouragement?" The answer is, "spirit of Jezebel."

He continues by saying, "Even though you stand against her lusts and witchcraft's, you must guard against the *power demons of fear and discouragement*; for these she will send against you to distract you from your warfare and your victory!" Notice he calls fear and discouragement "power demons." Fear sounds an alarm to run, panic, or seek death as a way out. I had two male relatives that committed suicide and I almost fell under this spell of death when I feared living this life and facing battles I felt I could not overcome. But God... in His word calls us to be conquerors and overcomers and I believed Him. Do you?

Control defined: To exercise authority or influence over, to dominate, pilot or steer, to rule. Only God has authority over heaven and earth. (Matt. 28:18). God alone rules and reigns over all men. He is not a co-pilot; He is all sufficient on His own. If you recognize this spirit of control operating in your own personal life, repent and pray that God will remove its stronghold.

Jezebel feeds on fear: I have experienced the spirit of Jezebel moving in churches to the point where the pastor was afraid to use his God-given authority in his own church. (Luke 10:19). As a matter of fact,

I have heard testimonies from pastors who actually left the church or was fired because of these spirits operating in their church. Eventually, the pastor either had to sell his church and step down. It moves throughout the staff as well as the congregation. We should always pray for our pastors and leaders. Watchman and intercessors usually discern when this spirit is overwhelming in a congregation and will pray through to victory. I bought a book called, "Exposing Witchcraft in the Church" written by one of my favorite pastors, Rick Godwin. The Lord told me to buy a copy for one of my pastors' years ago.

THE POWER OF PRAYER

Many times, during my own wilderness experiences undergoing great oppression, I would seek the Lord. The word of God says those who seek the Lord will find Him. Years ago when I was attending a church service, a spirit of heaviness came upon me because of personal problems. The Lord then told me to "Enter into his rest." I told him I did not know how. I had been fighting battles for so long; I did not know how to rest. He settled my spirit through the word and praise and worship. God has an answer in Isaiah 61:3. One of my favorite psalms in prayer during times of trial is Psalm 18. (See 2 Sam. 22). This was King David's prayer of deliverance.

King Hezekiah: A bad report of threats came to King Hezekiah from Rabshakeh in 2 Kings Chapters 18 and 19. Isaiah gave a word of encouragement from the Lord to not be afraid because of the words he had heard the servants of the King of Assyria who blasphemed the Lord. Hezekiah's prayer went up before the Lord. (2 Kings 19:15-19). When this leader's back was against the wall, he sought the God of Israel. After the Lord sent word through Isaiah, in the night the Angel of the Lord went out and struck 185,000 Assyrians in their camp. (2 Kings 19:35). Hezekiah overcame through the power prayer and the Angel of the Lord delivered Jerusalem. (2 Kings 19:35). Later, Hezekiah prayed for deliverance from death and the Lord extended his life fifteen (15) years. (2 Kings 20:6).

We have all experienced receiving bad reports. They come to us personally and through threats from other nations; and when it does, fear, anxiety and panic sets in. When it happens, we must remember that Jesus encourages us to pray. (Matt. 21:22). Prayer is powerful and I will talk about the gift of intercession later on in the text. (Read Eph. 1:18-23).

Moses and the people of Israel's journey through the wilderness is symbolic of man's struggles and experiences in life with God's presence and authority. We may grumble and complain about our neighbors or our leaders, but God is always there to listen and instruct us along the way. We can all look forward to God's promises for His kingdom is our Promise Land and the word of the Lord carries us there.

FEAR AND IDOLATRY

When you dominate, control, or manipulate a person's life or practice any kind of mind-control, you are replacing God's will with self. The word of God says in life or death, we belong to the Lord. (Rom. 14:8). We were bought with a price. (I Corin. 6:19-20). (Luke 20:38).

He is life to us. (Acts 17:28).

Fear can bring on a spirit of idolatry. In Ex. 32:1-4 we see where fear of the unknown can lead to idolatry. Moses was delayed coming down from Mount Sinai, so the people of Israel made a golden calf. When people get tired of waiting on God, they tend to take matters into their own hands for fear that either nothing will happen at all or the outcome will not satisfy their own self-will. I am guilty of a lack of trust on God's part to come through for me in certain situations. God is helping me to overcome this lack of trust by replacing fear with faith and standing on His word to back Him up. What is the golden calf in your life? Moses was seeking God on the people's behalf, but they could not wait, so they turned to other gods (idols). While God was planning their future by setting down laws and judgments and letting them know what He expected of them, they were busy shaping and molding gods of their own. Matters really began to worsen when they started soliciting other people to participate. We must wait on the Lord. (Isa. 40:31).

The Lord saw the great evil being done while Moses was on the mount and told Moses to get down there for the people were corrupting themselves. The Lord said they have turned aside quickly out of the way which I commanded them: they have made a molten calf, and worshipped it, and have sacrificed unto it. They credited the idol for delivering them out from the land of Egypt and kindled the wrath of the Lord so He told Moses He indeed have seen that these people were stubborn. Then the Lord wanted to be alone with His wrath so He could destroy them. (Ex. 32:8-10). Moses entreats the Lord on their behalf. What an intercessor!

Fear can change our behavior and cause us to

act irrational as in the case of the golden calf and in the case of King Saul. In I Samuel 13:8, King Saul made the same mistake when he was tired of waiting for the prophet Samuel to return. Fear took hold when he saw the people scattering because of Samuel's delay in returning. He took the position of priest and made an offering. When Samuel arrived, he told Saul that he acted foolishly and disobeyed God's commands. He also said that his kingdom would not endure. We pay a price for our actions.

This is what happens when we are impatient in waiting on a word from the Lord. Leaders must pray for the fruit of patience. Otherwise, we begin to worship self and exalt ourselves by replacing God's will with our own. The Lord chose Saul to be king; not a position of priest.

Don't give up. People will disappoint you but continue to seek the Lord on their behalf like Moses. Any man who can cry out to the Lord in such a way that God's heart is turned and His anger lessened is a man after God's own heart. How did Moses accomplish this? He reminded the Lord of His word and promise to Abraham, Isaac, and Jacob. The Lord cannot deny Himself so He changed His mind. (Exodus 32:12-14).

Moses asked Aaron what happened that the people

had such an influence over him which caused him to bring such sin upon the people. Aaron's response to Moses was to not lose his temper, for he knew what these people were like that they were likely to do evil deeds. The question was never answered. Sounds like excuses we make in order to pass responsibility on to some else. Are you allowing people to influence you to do evil? Are you the kind of leader who, like Aaron, allows people to get out of control? (Ex. 32:21-24).

We build golden calves in our hearts when our heart's desire is for the things of this world. It is symbolic of the worship of material possessions rather than God. We build golden calves when we would rather adhere to the words of the world instead of the truth of God's word. We make the wrong offerings to the Lord like Cain and Saul when we refuse to listen to the voice of the Lord, fear man, and grow impatient.

Moses then stood in the gate of the camp and gave the people a choice. Whoever decided to come to the Lord's side were to approach Moses. There will come a time in your life when you will have to make that same choice. After all was said and done, the people who were on the Lord's side executed judgment on the others as Moses instructed. Three thousand men fell that day. Are you prepared to do the will of God even when it means going against family, co-workers, and friends? Jesus spoke about choices in Matthew 10:37. Our love for God must exceed that of our own family. We must take up our cross and follow Him.

Fear and idolatry in some instances can work hand in hand when we start to focus on self and pleasing people. We submit to what we fear. Don't give your power away by allowing a person(s) or circumstance to take control over your will. No one is bigger and more powerful than God. Do not allow words to defeat you. Remember Hezekiah, who after receiving the enemies words against the God of Israel, sought the Lord and sent his servants to the prophet Isaiah to request prayer for the remnant of Israel. The Lord's answer through Isaiah promised deliverance.

When the servants of Hezekiah went to Isaiah, he gave word from the Lord to not be afraid of the words (threats) which were heard from the servants of the King of Assyria who blasphemed the Lord. He continued to say that the Lord would place a spirit in him to hear a rumor and return to his own land and there the Lord would cause him to fall by the sword. (2 Kings 18:26-37; 2 Kings 19:1-7). Fear was defeated by the word of the Lord!

Paul writes in Galatians 5:19-20 that sorcery, strife, dissensions, and idolatry, etc. are works of the flesh; and in verse 21 he says that those who choose to follow this path will lose their kingdom inheritance. The word of God is truth and we have a great intercessor, Jesus Christ, who is head over every power and principality, rule, and authority. (Col. 2:9-10).

As people of God we must rise up in prayer. (2 Corin. 10:5). We can either be overcomers through Christ, or we can be overcome by fear. It is our choice; therefore, submit to God, fight and oppose the devil that he may flee from your midst.

FEAR POURS OUT LIES

Fear can very easily become a foundation for lies. Let's go back to the book of Genesis. Abram fears for his life, so he tells Sarai to lie about being his wife.

In Genesis 12:11-20, when Abram was about to enter into the land of Egypt, he said to Sarai his wife that he realized she was beautiful to behold so when the Egyptians recognizes this fact, they will say to themselves, "This is his wife" and will kill me but allow you to live. He begged her to tell them that she was his sister so that all would go well with him and her. When Pharaoh took her into his house, God gave Abram favor with the Egyptians and provided for his family in verse 16. What became of this lie? Sickness and anger broke out in the land of Egypt. God struck Pharaoh and his house with great plagues because of Sarai, Abram's wife. Pharaoh's eyes were opened to the truth about Sarai and he confronts Abram about the deception. "Why did you not tell me that she was your wife?" Abram was so concerned about his own welfare; it never entered his mind about what the consequences of this action would be.

FEAR IN MARITAL RELATIONSHIPS

Marriage is a very common milieu for the spirit of fear. I have personally experienced this spirit of fear and control, not only in my own marriage but I have also seen the effects that it has had on many other couples throughout the Body of Christ. In today's atmosphere of wife and child abuse, it can be very destructive.

The abusive wife has a low self-esteem and fears the abuse will only lead to more abuse and divorce. They love their husbands so deeply that they are willing to endure it and refuse to leave for their own personal reasons (maybe for the children and financial support, etc.). In my own marriage, I did not have any children, but I deeply loved my husband and as a Christian, did not believe in divorce. (Malachi 2:16). Divorce is like having a death in the family.

My husband was very controlling. He forced me to do things I would not ordinarily do on my own; for example like going into debt. I had to hold back tears because he dared me to cry. I experienced a lot of oral abuse. A pastor at a church I use to attend years ago said oral abuse was worse than physical abuse.

The Lord woke me up in the middle of the night to show me a phone number of where my husband was staying that night. A woman answered the phone asking who I was. I told her I was his wife and she told him to wake up and then gave the phone to him. He was immediately surprised to say the least and came on home. Husbands always fear their wives would find out the truth. Guilt brings on fear. Wives fear losing their husbands but no one should have to live a lie.

My husband committed adultery and left me after five and a half years. God warned me of the deception and my spirit feared the outcome because by then my marriage was in real jeopardy. My husband phoned me one Sunday when I had just come back from a church service to ask me for a divorce. Right after the divorce the Lord spoke to me and said, "What are you crying about? He committed adultery with Me as well." He also said that from then on He would be my husband and He would take care of me. The Lord and I have been married for over 20 years and we are still going strong in love and laboring together. He has been my greatest love, encourager and provider.

We often try to control situations either by becoming argumentative, jealous, bitter, unforgiving, resorting to retaliation, or sometimes even violence. I thank God that wasn't my case. It never came to that. Instead, my husband and I, upon departing, declared our deep love for one another. I have not heard from him in over 20 years. I pray he is well and walking with the Lord.

My emotions were completely damaged as if I had taken out this whole ordeal on myself. In addition to that, I had Job friends that only made my situation worse with negative thoughts and opinions. For about 6 years I was in despair and, like Saul, did not hear from the Lord until one Sunday in church. A man of God came to me and prophesied a word of encouragement from the Lord about my situation. All we need is a word; a healing and restoring word from God. I was on my way back to my healing and living a normal life. Next, God told me to get away from people and get with Him in worship. I went to music stores praying over tapes and CDs and picked out my worship. This music is so anointed. The Spirit of God told me to choose tapes of people who were not famous and He chose this tape by a woman I never heard of before. When I read the label inside the tape, there was a statement made that said it was produced through much prayer and fasting. This and other worship CDs and my willingness to obey God in this matter led to my total healing in the years ahead. Now we know why God told Moses and Pharaoh to bring His people to His Mountain to worship Him. Worship brings the presence of God closer to our hearts, removes us from the bondage of the past, and heals us of our wounds and distress.

I blamed the Lord and myself because after the divorce, the Lord told me that he was the man He had chosen for me but because of his adultery, the marriage failed. A pastor from Dallas prophesied over me months later and said that my husband didn't just leave me, he left the anointing of God. My husband was called of God to be a pastor.

The truth of God's word in James 3:16 says that wherever envy, jealousy, and confusion exist, evil abounds. Thank you Lord for an amicable release.

Be prayerful, trust God to deliver, stand still and see the salvation of the Lord. His word must always rule over marital relationships. It all boils down to **trust**. This trust we can only get from a risen Lord.

We will never be afraid. (Isa. 12:2).

In a Christian marriage, a husband, wife, and God are in a covenant relationship. Worship God, pray together, and study to show yourself approved by God. Be a doer of the word, not just hearers only.

ADAM AND EVE

Let's go back to another book of the bible to the first married couple and see how disobedience to the word of God gives rise to fear. (See Gen. 3:8-13).

When Adam and Eve realized they had sinned they hid themselves. We hide when we fear the presence of God because of our guilt and shame. An intercessor told me years ago that God crucified shame on the cross. Fear gains a foothold when we know we are guilty of an act and have to come clean about it. As long as our sins are hidden, we are safe from any lecture or discipline. God called to Adam and said, "Where are you?" Adam responded by saying to God that he heard Him in the Garden and he was afraid because he was naked. God then asked him to reveal who it was that told him he was naked and continued to ask if he was disobedient and ate of the tree he commanded him not to eat.

Adam said Eve, the woman God gave to him, gave him the fruit from the tree. Fear finds other avenues to deflect personal liability. In other words, when people don't like the way conversations lead to the truth, avoidance takes hold because right now, all roads lead to me. Once truth is revealed, we look for someone other than ourselves to blame. Adam came to the conclusion that because God created Eve for him, He and she were the source of his own actions of disobedience. God spoke as a command to Adam first about the tree. Excuses and blame are born out of fear. Then God spoke to the woman asking her what had she done? We have the same scenario, Eve said that the serpent deceived her, and she ate. Ears should come with spiritual radar that detects all lies and blame and sounds the alarm when we miss the mark. Deception is no excuse for disobedience. Both Adam and Eve received the command from God. (See Gen. 2:17).

Alas, God called down judgment on all three: Adam, Eve, and the serpent. We all know the consequences of their actions. (Gen. 3:22-24). We make it even harder on ourselves when we turn a deaf ear to God. If you want God's approval, listen to His word and follow through with action. (2 Tim. 3:14-17).

Today, some pastors, people in ministry, and secular leaders are unwilling to accept the truth about God speaking through the person of the Holy Spirit. The fear of hearing the voice of God gives control over to the flesh (the carnal man). Through personal testimony later on in the text, you will see how God has spoken to me on numerous occasions, and how His voice (through His Spirit) assisted me in overcoming personal fears of my own.

Just like Adam and the people of Israel, there are many people today who fear the voice of God. Take it from someone who has heard His voice, it has saved my life on numerous occasions and have comforted me when no one else would. Just pray and quietly listen for His still small voice as a Shepherd calling to His sheep. The call is for everyone with no exceptions.

OBEDIENCE TO GOD'S WORD THROUGH BATTLES

Obedience is the key to receiving favor with God and achieving peace with our enemies. (Ex. 11:3; 12:35-36). God will make even your enemies to be at peace with you. (Prov. 16:7). This is especially important for those in leadership positions. God desires obedience, which is better than sacrifice. (I Sam. 15:22; Jer. 7:23). "Moses did all that God commanded."

In Exodus 14:8-10, after the Israelites left Egypt, the Lord hardened the heart of Pharaoh, who then pursued the Israelites. When Pharaoh drew near, the Israelites looked up and saw the Egyptians marching after them. They were extremely frightened so they cried out to the Lord.

They then took their eyes off God and began to speak words of doubt, unbelief, and fear of death.

But Moses shouted, "Fear not!" He encouraged them to stand still for they would see the salvation of the Lord; furthermore, the Lord would not only fight their battle but give them rest. What an encouraging word to give someone who is in fear for their lives. [God is speaking to us today as a reminder of what Moses said to the people of Israel. We must not fear the battles of this life but instead trust and take our rest in the Lord]. The Lord responds as though Moses knew better than to cry out to Him. God is moved by faith. It is all about faith and trust. He told Moses to just tell them to go forward. The Red Sea was parted for the Israelites to cross over to freedom on the other side. When trouble comes your way, take the advice Moses gave to the children of Israel when Pharaoh pursued them in the wilderness. Trust in the Lord. (Ex. 14:14).

Over the years, we have heard time and time again, "Fear is the opposite of faith." I agree. Jesus spoke of faith in measures in the New Testament. "Oh ye of *little faith*" in Matt. 6:30; and great *faith* in Matt. 8:10. It is in the heat of battle that the Lord looks to the person of faith and says, "Go forward!"

The Lord led me through a time of battle in 1995. I had battles with my health, my job, and my marriage--all at the same time. Many of my brothers and sisters in Christ asked, "What can we do for you?" I replied, "Just pray." God was taking me through a faith walk. After receiving no response from the Lord about my situations at the time, I asked a brother in Christ to go to the Lord on my behalf. After seeking the Lord on my behalf, he told me that the Lord responded in this manner: "Do not interfere, this is between her and me." I knew then that He was taking me on a walk of faith. Somehow I grew stronger during that time.

One of the battles I fought took place in the office. At the time, a supervisor who had lied on my evaluation was persecuting me on my job. He defamed my character and tried to destroy my reputation. Since I was a good employee who always did my job, he never commented on my work ethic. I had initially tried to bring this man to court, but the Lord sent word to me through a sister in Christ. He told her to tell me, "This is not the time to fight. Trust me to cover you; I am your Defender." I was upset at this word, but I obeyed. Later, I received an interoffice memorandum from this same supervisor, revising a lower standing on this same evaluation to a higher upgrade. A copy was sent to my personnel file. I was hoping that the memorandum package was a layoff notice, but the Lord did not let me take the easy way out. I continued to work for this man until the Lord transferred me to another department shortly thereafter. Complaints about this supervisor from others within the company prompted me to continue praying for this individual's salvation.

It takes great faith to believe God to remove fear from our lives. Fear and unbelief walk hand in hand. Earlier, the serpent deceived Eve into believing a distortion of the truth of the word of God. (See Gen. 3:1). I see the tree in the Garden as every temptation known to man that oppose the will of God. When doubt enters into our thoughts, we are in jeopardy of losing our blessing. Doubt cancels out faith and trust. (James 1:7-8). When we start to question the word of God, we are in doubt and unbelief. God means what He says.

One Saturday morning as I was walking to the grocery store, the Lord spoke to me. He said, "My people are walking in unbelief, they are not walking in the victory I have given them." I will never forget how grieved my spirit was on hearing that word.

Obedience helps you to keep your healing as expressed in Exodus 15:26. After my divorce, I continually prayed that the Lord would remove self-pity, rejection, heaviness, unforgiveness, resentment, and a spirit of abandonment far from me. Months later, the Lord told me to repent of my self-righteous attitude towards my husband and that I was not his pastor. So I did as He commanded and admitted to my husband that I failed in this area. Four years later, the Lord healed my body and my emotions. He delivered me from the persecution I had encountered at work. Victory in my body came first, subsequently, my job. God is so faithful; His promises are true. He opened up the Red Sea for me just as He did for His children back then. With God taking the lead, you have already won the victory.

GOD A MIGHTY WARRIOR

The Lord told Moses that He would not cross the Jordan. Moses summoned Joshua and said to him in the presence of all Israel. Be strong and courageous, for you must move forward as the Lord commanded to the land that He swore to give to your forefathers and divide the land as an inheritance. (Deut. 31:7). I love the integrity of Moses. He encouraged Joshua not to be afraid and spoke to him in the assembly where all of Israel could witness his words of reassurance. There is authenticity and confirmation in relinquishing an office to a chosen leader in front of his followers. No one would be able to question who would take lead after Moses. I encourage you today that whatever you are going through, remain strong and courageous, for the Lord goes before you to hold you up in your position of leadership.

Joshua: God is a great military strategist. Joshua was aware of this fact even before the walls of Jericho came down. He saw many signs and wonders from the Lord while standing side by side with Moses. His loyalty to both God's leadership and Moses' won him many battles in the end; especially the battle with Jericho. (Joshua 6:1-16). Good leaders will know and trust their replacement when their time to lead is ended. Joshua was such a man.

Moses knew that God would not forsake His people even before the parting of the Red Sea. Surround yourself with encouraging people who will lift you up and speak faith in times of crisis. A great leader inspires his people to advance when they want to quit or has a tendency to fall back into bondage. (Exodus 14:10-14). They believed God, obeyed Him, and were triumphant over their enemies. It doesn't matter whether you are a General in the world's army or a warrior in the army of God, you can boldly say that no enemy will rule over us if God be for us. (Rom. 8:31).

After the Lord delivered His people from Pharaoh's army, they sang a song to the Lord. We need to praise God always (whether He delivers us or not). The Lord inhabits (lives in) the praises of

His people. King Jehoshaphat, through praise and worship, defeated the people of Ammon, Moab, and Mount Seir. (2 Chron. 20:1-30). Surely it has always been said that our deliverance is in the praise.

Through Jesus Christ, let us stir our hearts to never cease from continually offering up to God our praise, being unafraid to confess His name and becoming witnesses to everyone we may encounter. (Heb. 13:15). Why? The answer is found in Hebrews 13:6. We can say with confidence and most assuredly that God is our Helper and we shall not fear man nor any of his devices that may come against us. Needless to say, there is no one I would rather have on my side in a battle than the Lord. (Heb. 10:30-31).

Then Moses and the Israelites sang this song to the Lord, which included:

- An exaltation and praise to the Lord.
- They declared that God is: "Their Strength, their Song, their Salvation, their God and Father, their Warrior."
- His mighty works.
- His eternal reign.

How wonderful it is to praise the Lord!

Deliverance is in the praise. Notice, however, that immediately after the Lord delivered His people, the grumbling begins. Do you ever praise the Lord on Sunday and grumble on Monday?

Obedience brings healing. (Ex. 15:26).

This is where the Lord declares that if His people will hear His voice and obey His statutes, He will put none of the diseases on them. He then declares that He is the Lord their Healer. He makes us whole physically and spiritually.

The Lord commands the people of Israel to rest on the Sabbath. During the summer of 1995, the Lord revealed to me that He set aside the Sabbath day for people who need rest from the week's battles and people who feel unclean and needed to be cleansed. We are cleansed through the word of God, the blood of the Lamb, and prayer. This is why He set this day aside.

Yet some people refuse to worship the Lord on the Sabbath. Here is a common excuse that will sound very familiar. "People who worship on the Sabbath are hypocrites. They go to church on Sunday and raise hell all week." I have heard this time and time again over the years and it stands to reason that this is why we go to church in the first place. Here are five reasons to worship the Lord.

First and foremost: God is our Creator, King, and Lord, and He deserves our worship and praise.

Second: It is a command from God for His daily provision. (Ex. 16:28-30). It also brings forth his presence in our midst.

Third: It is an act of honor and respect for God and humbles us to submit to His will and command placing Him in His rightful above ourselves.

Fourth: It nurtures fellowship with the Father and with other people in the Body of Christ.

Fifth: It declares who God is and what He is able to do for us.

HELP AND SUPPORT

[Ex. 17:10-13 "The conflict with Amalek"].
Joshua, in obedience to Moses, fought against
Amalek. The signs of a future leader are to submit
to one the one he has. During this conflict, as long
as Moses held his hands up, Israel prevailed. A high
hand is a symbol of military power and praise to
God. When Moses' hands grew tired, Aaron and
Hur held them up for him. We all need one another
for support. Leaders get tired also; they could use
our support. My pastor stated once that he wasn't
the only minister, we are all ministers in the Lord.

On another occasion when I was going through
a very difficult battle; the Lord said to me, "This is
for all burden bearers--Pick up your cross and follow
me. I had to carry My cross alone, but you have the
Word, the Holy Spirit, and each other." I never

forget words the Lord has spoken to me over the years. It has sustained me through many battles.

Moses told his father-in-law Jethro all that the Lord had done to deliver his people from Pharaoh. (Ex. 18:8). Are you testifying of the greatness of God and how He delivered you? A good leader will glorify God and tell of His marvelous works. A great leader will also listen to the wisdom of others (Godly wisdom). The word of God will bear witness to the witness of the wisdom of others. Jethro saw that Moses was overworked and that he would wear himself out eventually if he did not seek assistance. (Ex. 18:17-23). Moses listened to his father-in-law's advice. (Verses 24-26). A leader should not be afraid or too prideful to ask for help from others. I had a precious pastor named Bill Love many years ago. He has gone to be with the Lord. He, like Moses, tried to do all the work and labor at his church when the Lord told him to ask for help. (Prov. 11:14).

MOSES RECEIVES THE TEN COMMANDMENTS

Although we are under grace now and not the law, Jesus said that We should not think that He came to destroy the law or the prophets but to fulfill. (Matt. 5:17-19). God's laws are still valid today. In the past few years, there have been certain individuals and groups whose sole purpose was to take the Ten Commandments off of buildings and other places in our communities in America. In verse 19 Jesus said that those who would want to annul even one of the least of the commandments and try to convince others to do the same shall be called least in the kingdom of heaven. On the other hand, those who would preserve and hold on to them shall be called great in the kingdom of heaven.

There is a sermon in each of these commandments. The Ten Commandments keeps us in agreement with

God's will for our lives and safety. They build integrity and character and a more excellent spirit. (See I John 3:22). God gave Moses His commandments on the mountain to preserve and protect His people from ever getting into the sin of bondage ever again. It demonstrated a lifestyle God wanted His people to follow in pleasing Him.

1. We shall worship no other gods but the God of Israel. (Ex. 20:2-3). I have included the words of Jesus that no servant can serve two masters. (Luke 16:13).

2. We should not create or build anything in an image or likeness of a god that is in heaven, earth, or in the waters of the earth. (Ex. 20:4-6). Pray for a life free from idolatry.

3. We are never to take the Lord's name in vain. (Ex. 20:7). (See also Lev. 22:32).

4. We must keep His Sabbath day holy. (Ex. 20:8-11). As stated earlier, praise brings deliverance and it is where God abides. The Lord blessed the Sabbath day and hallowed it. (Ex. 20:11). He only asks for one day out of the week. What better way to honor Him. He redeemed mankind from their transgressions and iniquities, seated us in

heavenly places, and gave us eternal life. All creation should praise, worship, and glorify Him as Lord, Savior, and Creator of all mankind. We are not to profane the Sabbath. (See also Isa. 56:6).

5. We must honor our parents that we may have a long life in the land. (Ex. 20:12). (See also Eph. 6:1-3). We would not be here at all if it were not for moms and dads. They may not be perfect, but then, who is? They are our providers, counselors, and protectors.

6. We should not kill anyone. (Ex. 20:13). God is the Creator of life. He is the "Bread of Life." (Prov. 8:35-36). He is a God of the living. Murder, in this context, includes spiritual as well as physical. (I John 3:15).

7. We shall not commit adultery. (Ex. 20:14). There are three kinds of adultery: (1) Jesus spoke about adultery by intent (lustful eyes). (Matt. 5:28); (2) Israel committed adultery when they went seeking after other gods. (Idolatry); and (3) breaking a vow in a marriage covenant. (Heb. 13:4).

8. We shall not steal. (Ex. 20:15). We must determine in our hearts not to steal from

anyone but in labor may have something to share with those in need. (Eph. 4:28).

9. We shall never bear false testimony against our neighbor. (Ex. 20:16). This is one of the things the Lord hates; a false witness who utters lies. (See Prov. 6:16-19). Lies can destroy a person's career and family. Many people, in past as well as present, have spent thousands of dollars in litigation suing one another for defamation and slander.

10. We shall not covet our neighbor's house, wife, or property. (Ex. 20:17). We have seen this spirit operating in people's marriages (adultery), in politics (coveting political positions), in corporations regarding promotions etc. There are two traits which, when generated in the spirit, can cause one to covet---jealousy and comparison. The Pharisees were envious of Jesus Christ. We envy what someone else possesses or compare what you have with what someone else has. (James 3:16). What God gives to us is for us alone and others, for their own benefit; so let us have a heart full of gratitude to the Lord.

11. Someone said once that every civilized law ever made was based on the

Ten Commandments. Robbery, murder, kidnapping, etc. are crimes, and people do get penalized. I once compared the Ten Commandments with the state's penal code and was amazed at the similarities.

ENTERING INTO GOD'S PRESENCE

The people who came to Mt. Sinai trembled with fear at the sound of the trumpet and thundering, and when they saw smoke. The people asked Moses to intercede to God on their behalf because they reasoned that if they spoke to God, they would die. (Ex. 20:18-19). Moses told them not to be afraid that God was testing them so they would fear Him and not sin against Him. When we are in fear we are to pray because God has not given us a spirit of fear. The way we should fear God is to revere (esteem, honor, adore) Him. It is a holy fear.

Fear (depending on the circumstances) can sometimes keep you from entering into His presence. Fear can hinder your prayer life.

They asked Moses to intercede on their behalf.

Fear and sin are sometimes synonymous as explained earlier (disobedience).

Every leader should be able to hear from God. How do you know when you are truly hearing from God? If what you hear lines up with the word of God, you know it is from Him. You must first be born again and be baptized in the Holy Spirit. There are many channels through which God speaks and ministers to us, but they are all related to prayer, the Word, and the gifts of the Spirit. Many modern-day Christians don't acknowledge these gifts. It is not so much that they don't believe in them or don't want to receive them as it is that they fear having them. I was the same way years ago.

Some of the gifts of the Spirit are listed in I Corin. 12:7-11.

Desire a pure heart of love as well as the gifts of the Spirit. (I Corin. 14:1).

God has spoken to me through so many people during times when I was under spiritual attack and oppression. They have prayed and encouraged me in the Lord. During my wilderness experiences, He sent people to prophesy over me and give me words of wisdom and knowledge, all of which have come to pass. He is our hope of glory.

BUILDING
GOD'S HOUSE

A great leader will use discretion and discernment when choosing church leaders, business associates, friends, a mate, or acquaintance. They will not be influenced by popular opinion. They should be men who fear God and have a heart of truth who hate dishonest gain. (Ex. 18:21). They will not be influenced by popular opinion. They should not associate with evil people or bear witness with people who pervert justice. (Ex. 23:2). (See also Psm. 1:1-3). Only God can examine the motives of a heart. (I Corin. 4:5). God will expose things that are hidden in the dark. (Matt. 10:26). In my own prayer life, God had found things that were hidden from me on several occasions over the years.

Moses was on the mountain forty days and forty nights. During this time, the Lord gave cubit-by-cubit instructions on how to build His tabernacle (i.e. colors, types of wood, and other countless details). Pastors are you seeking the Lord's guidance on how to build the Body of Christ or how to plan His worship service? Do you seek the Lord on whom to choose as deacon or elder? When you continually seek the Lord and His word, He will instruct you on how He expects you to build both His temple as well as your own. We must allow God to do the building. (Psm. 127:1). A great leader will seek wisdom from above.

David said that he would hide God's word in his heart that he might not sin against Him. (Psm. 119:11). The apostle Paul stated what God had said in Genesis 1:31. *Everything that God created is good* and he added that nothing is to be refused if it is received with a grateful heart; for it is sanctified by the way of God's word and prayer. This includes sanctification of our churches and our own temples. A leader who has this vision of God's creation will love everyone regardless of race, sex, or religious preference. Do you judge people by their appearance? (See James 2:2-4).

CONDEMNATION

One day when I was in my kitchen cleaning dishes, the Spirit of God spoke to me about Romans 8:1. He said we should not condemn ourselves, no one should condemn us, and we should not condemn others. This verse of scripture is inclusive. Leaders will have to be able to overcome the fear condemnation by the people close to them.

The very people Moses led out of Egypt, including his own sister Miriam grumbled and spoke against him. They even went so far as to question his leadership abilities, yet Moses continued to stand in the gap and pray to God on their behalf. The word of God says we are not to gripe or murmur against one another unless we be condemned for the Judge stands at the door. (James 5:9).

In my own life, God has spoken to me on many

occasions. It was usually for my own education and edification; sometimes it was for correction and clarification of the Word. He also speaks this way to the Body of Christ. We need to know God's heart, His plan, and purpose for His people. When we ask according to His will, He hears us. (I John 5:14). But how are we to know His will unless we inquire of Him or go to His word? In John 6:38, Jesus expressed the fact that He did not come by His own will but by the will of the Father.

In 1984, I was offered a job. During my interview, they asked if I had experience in accounting and budgeting. I had no degree or experience. My fear was like a self-condemnation. I felt I did not have what it takes so therefore I would not be hired. I did not want to even answer the question because I had absolutely no background or experience in these particular fields. I was sincere in saying I had not but was willing to learn. Before accepting the job, I asked the Lord for wisdom, knowledge, and understanding of these particular skills. After about six years in that one position, the supervisor of accounting said that I kept the best records in the company. God determines our worth, not man.

I give all the glory to God. God shows us how He is able to give us wisdom in all sorts of skills. (Ex. 31:3).

Once God fills you with His Spirit, you will never be the same again. We are able to accomplish tasks that are above our own knowledge and skill. We should all work towards serving the Lord, and once we realize who our real employer is, we will cease to grumble and complain about our own situation or anyone else's and we will have the confidence to boldly take on positions where we feel we are inept. (Phil. 4:6-7).

God is perfect. A great leader directs his attention and that of the people under his care to God. We are all accountable to God. A good shepherd prays for his flock.

THE FEAR OF CORRECTION AND DISCIPLINE

Disciples have the word 'discipline' in it. As Disciples of Christ, leaders are expected to correct and discipline their flock. We must carry out scripture for this purpose found in 2 Timothy 3:16 which includes and is not limited to correction and rebuke. In saying that, we are to admonish and not abuse our authority.

When leaders placate their flock, it only serves to stimulate them to usurp their authority. They see you in a weak light; taking advantage of every situation and seizing an opportunity to micromanage. The people of Israel took advantage of Moses by condemning and accusing him. They placed blame on him for their conditions in the wilderness regarding provision. It is impossible to make everyone happy. You can do everything possible to help them, like Moses, and they will still continue to try you and test you.

I have always counseled my people. If I had a problem with an individual, I counseled with them privately. If two or in a group, I would counsel them as well. I have encountered jealousy and favoritism inside my congregation. There were also a lot of backbiting and deception. Whatever spirit is operating that is not godly at the time, if you are too timid to speak, ask God for a sermon of conviction for all to hear as an alternative or for other instructions. There were many times when God changed the message of my sermon before it was given on Sunday. Leaders of nations normally call for a press or peace conference in the midst of turmoil. At those times, I call upon the Lord and take counsel with Him. He will always have your back.

Ezra 10:1-11: Ezra, a priest in charge of rebuilding the temple, was in prayer weeping bitterly before the Lord because the people had been unfaithful in marrying foreign women from the land. He called for a meeting and spoke to the men of Judah and Benjamin at Jerusalem. They were afraid and distressed because of the matter to be discussed.

He told them to confess their unfaithfulness to God, repent, and separate themselves from the people of the land. Correction is never easy for a leader; he needs God to take the lead.

A true leader and soldier in Christ will place God's command before anything and anyone else. It is the Lord's discipline, not ours that we are to convey. (Prov. 22:15). When we do find good behavior, we should do what the Apostle Paul did when he addressed the Colossian church; express our thankfulness, acknowledge and encourage others to continue on in good discipline. (Col. 2:5-6).

Because Moses had a very powerful prayer life, the Lord initiated and followed through with disciplining the people of Israel.

GOD REVEALS HIMSELF

A great leader will never tempt the Lord by saying, "He is not in the midst of us." (Ex. 17:7). No matter how difficult your circumstance or situation, Jesus promised that He would never leave us or forsake us. What could Pharaoh do to God's people? Even after they saw the hand of God move against their enemies time and time again and repeatedly provided them with meat and bread in the wilderness, they still doubted. God has proven his faithfulness to me many times in past years. God has proven Himself faithful to all of us by suffering and dying on the cross for our sins. Are we still crucifying Him?

God reveals Himself to Moses in another way in Exodus 17:8-16: "The Lord is My Banner." Joshua was a leader in battle but it was only through God that the war was won. Everyone knew the victory came from the Lord. Good leaders, refrain from striving to win the war in their own flesh, but give the battle to the Lord. (I Sam. 17:46-47). Isn't it comforting to know that we don't have to fight our own battles?

After every battle, God reveals Himself in a new way. After one emotional and spiritual battle, God revealed to me how He has been my "Abba Father" from the time I was a child. My father was never home. As a World War II veteran, he lived mainly in

VA hospitals most of his life and when he was home he was out there in the night life. My mother was a single parent to my four sisters and myself while he was away. God has proven Himself faithful to me since birth and continues to do so today. I almost died as an infant from very serious convulsions. My mother went to three different doctors before finding one with a cure for my illness. The third doctor saved my life. I can't even imagine my mother's fear in searching for a cure for her baby.

God may reveal Himself during times of war or through wilderness experiences. It is during these times that He wants to refresh us with living waters. (See John 7:37-38).

THE GIFT OF INTERCESSION
AND GOD'S PRESENCE IN
WORSHIP

Moses again seeks the Lord for the sins of his people. If you are a leader, I encourage you to intercede on behalf of our congregation. My armor bearer would drive me to church so I could on Saturday nights. All of a sudden, we started having problems with flat tires. The pastor wanted to know what happened to us. I asked the pastor if he was praying for us to be safe every Saturday night and he said no. We never had a problem since.

I heard a pastor say once, "How can we touch earth if we first don't touch heaven?" Jesus said His house shall be a house of prayer. Not only our churches, but also, our bodies are houses of prayer. If you want God's hand to move on situations in your church family or in your own personal life, I urge you to either begin organizing prayer groups, or seek the Lord on your own. I have always believed in preventive prayer. I don't believe in waiting for the ax to fall before I get on my knees. Prayer coverage is so vital every day; especially in these last days.

Are you a workaholic? Are you fighting many battles in life? Are you loaded down with heavy responsibilities? There is good news! God says His presence is with us and He will give us rest. (Ex. 33:14). In knowing God and finding favor with Him, you receive the most precious gift in the universe, the gift of having God reveal His heart to you personally.

There were many times in the past when I prayed with prayer partners. I would say, "Let's see what is on God's heart today." We will then begin to pray in the spirit for a while and you would be surprised how God shows us how to pray, and what to pray for. He also gives us vision, all at the same time. Once when we entreated the Lord in this fashion, I saw Him smile in the spirit. Jesus is such a precious Savior. If you pray in this way with a sincere heart, God will show you His character.

The Lord proclaims His mercy and forgiveness. (Ex. 34:6-7). Personal and private praise and worship shows respect for God and honor the relationship one shares with Him. *Praise and worship is prayer.* Moses hurriedly bowed his head and worshipped God. (Ex. 34:8). Humility should fill a leader's heart. If we really knew God, who He is, His character, His power, His mercy, and His loving kindness, we would run to the throne room in prayer, praise and worship. A good church home will invite the fellowship of other believers to join in with you. Acknowledge His presence in your lives.

FEAR CAN HINDER GOD'S CALL

I always had a heart for the youth. I was hoping that God would call me into that particular ministry. One Sunday, in the summer of 1994, while in praise and worship, God called me to a "Deliverance Ministry." My first response was, "Oh no, Lord please! I can't fight devils and demons, I just can't do it!" Here was His response: "I know you can't, I will do it through you." I submitted myself to His authority and His will and since then, I have been amazed at how God delivers people through His word and intercessory prayer. After praying in the spirit and receiving a word of wisdom or knowledge from God for someone, I have seen people praise and dance before the Lord for half an hour. They cry tears of joy, shaking and falling to their knees. They would glorify God for His faithfulness in freeing them from sin and bondage. I thank God today for making me an intercessor for His people.

I am barren. I cried out for many years for God to give me a son but He told me one night as I lay on my bed, "These [the Body of Christ] are the children I have given you." Tears ran from my eyes as I wept in silence on my pillow. I love God and I love what He has done for me and for the sake of His people.

I once laid hands on a woman when God spoke to me. He said, "Long ago, He made known to her the call He had on her life but she did not obey." He told me to tell her to repent. I asked her to confirm this word and she did. I then asked her why she did not heed the call. She replied, "I was afraid of failure." (There's that dreaded fear again!). After she repented and asked God's forgiveness, I prayed that the devil would no longer interfere in God's plans for her life under the authority of Jesus Christ, and that the Lord would give her back what she had lost. God then said to me, "I have been waiting a long time for this day." Today, this young lady conducts monthly bible study classes in her apartment complex. She thought that no one would show but the Lord supernaturally brought people in her path.

She had a good attendance. Fear can hinder the call of God on your life.

Who are we to delay the plans and purposes of God? Is God waiting for you now to heed His call? Don't make Him wait any longer. You may have a call from God in your place of employment, church home, street ministry, missions, your family, neighborhood, or in some other capacity. Listen to the voice of God. The whole world is a mission field, even your own home. God needs laborers. (Matt. 9:37-38). No matter what your call, profession, or station in life, you can be a soul-winning leader for Jesus Christ.

Everyone in the Israelite community had their individual duties. Moses was God's chosen leader for the nation of Israel. Aaron was a prophet and head priest. Aaron's sons were priests in the tabernacle. (Ex. 29:44). Miriam was a prophetess. (Ex. 15:20). Jethro was priest of Midian. Joshua was an officer in the army. If you have a call of God on your life (and we all do), don't argue with God or make excuses. Do not kindle God's anger as Moses did. (See Exodus 4:10-14).

Jonah: Jonah refused to go to Nineveh when the Lord called him. (Jon. 1:1-3). Are you running from a call of God on your life? You cannot run from the Lord. He will find you. Jonah arose to flee to Tarshish from the presence of the Lord. No one can flee from the presence of the Lord. Psalm 139:7-8: We cannot escape God's Spirit. In life or death, He is with us.

Jonah disobeyed the word of the Lord and the Lord sent a great wind on the sea. As a result, not only Jonah but the mariners who also sailed with him on the ship were in peril. Your disobedience can cause others to suffer along with you. (Case in point: Aaron and the molten calf).

As I said earlier, everyone had his or her own work assignments. Do you have a heart that is stirred and a spirit that is willing? (Ex. 35:21). These were obedient people, who were bringing offerings and service unto the Lord. Even the women who were gifted as artisans and whose hearts were stirred with wisdom came to give service. (Ex. 35:26). Until we know how to serve, we will never be able to lead. I think Jesus said it best in Matt. 20:26-28. Jesus came to serve and we are not above the Master.

When God gives you an assignment, make sure it is completed. Don't do it half way or leave it partially finished. Remember whom you are working for.

When we are hired, it is usually to replace the last person who had your present position? I have--several times as a matter of fact. Every time I was transferred to another department, I always had quite a clean up job. These are just a few examples: Updating new information from the old, throwing information out, putting new data in, changing data to accommodate new software, converting files, filing old information, and re-evaluating working priorities, etc. It can take as long as one to two years in order to restore order from the last office worker. It takes patience and a lot of effort, especially if you want your work to run more smoothly and efficiently. Just imagine how God feels! God-given talent and abilities are not to be wasted or neglected. Do the best you can and always remember what kind of God you serve. He is always able to carry you through any position in life or through any fear you may have.

Receive God's wisdom. (I Corin. 1:25). Jesus knew the purpose for which His Father sent Him. He did not leave this world without accomplishing that which His Father sent Him to do. Complete His work without any fear of opposition or work load.

The apostle Paul: Press on through and fulfill the work of the Lord. Like Moses said, "Move forward!" Faith and endurance will help you to fight a good fight. (2 Tim. 4:5-7).

Fathers are leaders of their families. Jesus is the head over our earthly fathers. (Eph. 5:23). Wives are help-mates. Don' be too proud to ask or confide in her. Trust her to assist you in succeeding. (i.e. support, labor, prayer, loving you through it, etc.). Moses was a father and, as we have seen, a great leader and intercessor. He knew God so well that he changed God's mind when the people kindled God's anger. Moses listened to Jethro's (his father-in-law) counsel. He was not so prideful about his responsibility that he could not listen to counsel or ask for help. He obeyed all that God commanded and loved God's people even though they were far from perfect. Moses was very responsible. (See I Tim. 3:5). Moses knew how to seek the Lord for the answer; so as a result he was able to take care of the family of God. He listened for the voice of God and sought Him daily for instruction, vision, and purpose.

All of us are leaders. We all are responsible for our own lives, our families, the family of God, and those under our supervision, but also to one another as people on this planet. The gift of helps is for everyone whether we realize it or not.

SUMMARY

HOW TO ACQUIRE GREAT LEADERSHIP ABILITIES IN THE ABSENCE OF FEAR

- Become a great intercessor for yourself, your friends, your family, and even your enemies. Even Pharaoh sought Moses to intercede on his behalf. (Ex. 8:8; 8:28; 9:27 28; 10:17). Because Moses continually sought the Lord, he was successful in leading God's people according to God's will. Provision and healing was made on their behalf as well as Moses'. Continue earnestly in prayer. Pray that God will manifest the fruits of His beatitudes in your mind, body, soul, and spirit.

  (Matt. 5:3-12).

- Be humble enough to accept help from others when work overwhelms you.

- Obedience is our gift to God. Wisdom, success, healing, salvation, and deliverance are His gifts to us.

- Don't give in to fear but only maintain a reverent fear of God.

- Know who God is. Ask for a heart to know God.

  (See Jer. 24:7).

- Endure hardship as a good soldier. The battle is the Lord's; give it to Him. (See Mark 13:13; 2 Tim. 2:3-4).

- Speak good words. Bless and do not curse.

- Do not exalt yourself over God's people. (Ex. 9:17). A great leader is first a servant. You may ask, "How can a leader become a servant?" Look at the life of Jesus Christ and follow His example of washing His apostles' feet. (refer to Luke 22:24-27).

- Seek the wisdom of God. (James 1:5). The wisdom of the world cannot be compared to the wisdom of God. (I Corin. 1:18-25).

- Encourage and support others. (Phil. 2:3-4).

- Do your work without grumbling or complaining.

- Let God build your house, your temple (we are the temples of the Holy Spirit). Remain faithful to God. (See Heb. 3:4-6).

- Serve the Lord. It is the greatest privilege and honor you could ever receive.

- Love God and others. (I John 4:11-12). (I John 4:16). Love does not carry fear but the perfect love of Jesus Christ casts out all fears. (I John 4:18). If you know someone is living in fear, pray that God's love will be made perfect in them.

- Don't make excuses. Run your race and press on towards the prize knowing that God is with you helping you to accomplish your goal.

Great leaders are molded and shaped. This should be our prayer:

Shape and mold me O God as the Potter who molds the clay; for we are all the work of your hands. (Isa. 64:8).

THE MOST IMPORTANT QUALITIES OF A LEADER

They must be able to –

1. Be a man or woman of integrity and have an excellent character and spirit.

2. This is a hard one: Be patient.

3. Not give up in the midst of great opposition.

4. Be able to suffer rejection and reproach from people (like Moses).

5. Be humble enough to accept godly counsel.

6. Protect and support the people under their charge.

7. Show kindness towards their enemies.

8. Negotiate peace before going to war.

9. Face their enemies unafraid.

10. Serve the God of Israel and obey and abide in His word.

11. Intercede on behalf of their church or nation.

12. Let God's truth rule and reign in their heart.

13. Let no corruption be found in their heart.

14. Place the needs of others before themselves.

15. Do not seduce people to sin against God and correct them according to the discipline of the Lord.

16. Great leaders instruct and train future leaders like Joshua.

I know the above seems impossible but with God all things are possible. Everyone wants to be a leader without having to carry these kinds of burdens. You don't realize what you are getting yourself into until you have actually stepped into a leadership position.

No matter how intelligent, powerful, or rich we are, we will never be free from fear until we start fearing (reverent fear) someone who is wiser, richer, or more powerful. His name is Jesus Christ, King of Kings and Lord of Lords. Many of us think we are untouchable. We think we will be able to live forever, spend money forever, and stay healthy forever. [Read Jeremiah 9:23-24].

Now we have come to the most important qualities of good leadership. Success is measured on what Moses said in prayer. (Ex. 33:13). Moses went to the Lord in prayer to gain more knowledge of His character so that he would continue to find favor with Him. **SEEK TO KNOW WHO GOD IS.**

King David knew God. A breakdown of Psalm 27 proclaims:

God is my Light and my Salvation. *As a result, there is no fear.*

God is my Defense. (v. 1).

God is my Hiding Place. (v. 5).

He is my Mother and Father. (v. 10).

God is my Helper.

In Psalm 23 - The Lord is my Shepherd I shall not want.

David was a man who believed God to be all of the above and more. Even when King Saul sought to kill him, he continued to recognize and declare who his God is. Do you know God?

Moses fasted and sought the Lord for forty days. We should not grow weary in seeking God. When Moses came down from the mount, the skin of his face shone so brightly that the people were afraid to go near him. Note that in Matt. 5:16 Jesus encourages us to be a light for Him before all the earth that they may see our good works and may glorify our Father in heaven.

The Lord gave instructions to Moses for His people and we are all God's people, whether we are pastors, executives, scout leaders, politicians, presidents, kings, or leaders of nations. If you want God to show you how to lead His people, seek His presence and ask Him for vision and purpose on how to guide and direct the people under your leadership. How can you do this? In Matthew 26:41, Jesus said to watch and pray lest we enter into temptation. Ask God to instruct you on how to become a good leader. Watch and pray. Allow God to show you the areas in which you are lacking wisdom, knowledge, and understanding. Seek God's heart. Let God take the lead and He will direct you and give you revelation and insight into every circumstance.

It is never too late for God to place His love and life in you. All you have to do is receive. People may not understand what you're going through but God does.

Moses was a man under a great deal of pressure. Thousands of people depended on him to deliver them from bondage, to seek the Lord on their behalf, and to make provision in the desert. For years people complained and grumbled. Yet through all the battles, complaints, and disappointments, he was obedient and he never gave up. As a result, he gained favor with God, as God remained faithful to Moses and to His people.

FEAR AND ANXIETY

Fear sounds an alarm in our spirit and soul. It can be a real and present danger or a false alarm. Anxiety disorders are a common mental health problem in America. Many psychiatrists and psychologists have written books on this subject calling them disorders and sometimes recommend medication. Fear works with anxiety and can cause physical symptoms. The word of God in Philippians 4:6-7 tells us to be anxious for nothing; but instead place our prayers and petitions before Him. He will place a peace guard over our minds and hearts in Christ Jesus.

MY ENCOUNTERS WITH LEADERSHIP ROLES

As a child, I had low self-esteem and hardly any friends at all throughout High School. I never saw myself as a leader so the Lord placed me in situations testing me out for the role. The first was when I joined the U.S. Army Reserves. I was the first female in First Army to join a JAG unit in Massachusetts. My first leadership role was chosen for me by my drill sergeant as 'Platoon Leader.' in basic training at Ft. McClellan, Alabama.

The Lord then told me to move to Houston, Texas and not look back to Boston. Like Abraham, I stepped out in faith and arrived in Houston without a job and nowhere to live. I transferred to Third Army here and stayed in the Reserves. When God send you somewhere He always provides. God had a plan.

I joined the Church of Christ here in Houston and was chosen to head up the Prison Ministry--my second leadership role where I had in-debt studies in the word of God. It was a smooth transition and I was surprised at how comfortable I was in presenting my report before the staff at my church. I also headed up the Worship Ministry and worked closely with my pastor, Bill Love who went to be with the Lord years later.

I then worked for an Oil and Gas firm and we had bible study every week at lunch time in the conference room. I taught a few times and really enjoyed it. God grooms and trains us for something greater. We just have to submit to His leading. Be patient in the process and you will make progress.

I left the Army Reserves and the Lord placed me in a church where I utilized my prophetic gift. I also moved in the gift of prophecy for my pastor and the great congregation. During my tenure there, I continued my study in bible classes. It was then that God opened up Extended Hands of Jesus Ministry where I prayed for pastors and ministers. I believe in supporting church leaders. After 6 years, the Lord moved me to another church where I ministered on Saturday nights for a few years. It was there that I was ordained. This led me to move on after 6 years and to hold church every Sunday for about 7 years. I loved all my pastors and pray that I will see them again someday to see where God has taken them thus far as they labor in His kingdom.

Extended Hands of Jesus now has kingdom connections in the United States. We strive to help pastors and ministers and have resource materials for a variety of studies in the Body of Christ.

MY INNERMOST FEAR

I had claustrophobia, a fear of being alone in an elevator or being locked in a small room alone. In 1994, I was given a new job assignment. I was to collect the mail every morning for everyone in my division at my workplace. The post office was in the lobby downstairs. I first took my dolly down the escalator because I was not aware there was a freight elevator. Even after learning of the freight elevator, I would not use it because it was too confining and I feared that it would break down and I would be left alone. I began having panic attacks. I told myself, "What if it breaks down and I am locked in this small elevator by myself?" "I would just die!" The elevator was so small that it could only hold about three to four individuals comfortably.

One day I was chewed out by the security guard in the building for not taking the freight elevator as

I was told. Even though I told him about my fear, he insisted that using the escalator was dangerous. He said that it was safer for the people on the escalator who were ahead of me or behind me if I were to take the freight elevator instead. I tried avoiding this security guard, but was caught a second time. He gave me a final warning. Fear can make you rebellious; I had been disobedient. I had only one choice: pray and ask God to take the fear away. For eight months, I fearlessly took that freight elevator. The Lord freed me from my fear.

Two years later, I took a trip to Dallas to attend my nephew's high school graduation. I stayed about a week and returned on Wednesday, May 28th. Before I left for my vacation in Dallas, on Saturday, May 24th, I had been concerned about a warfare situation at church. It was very serious and affected my personal life as well as the lives of people in the Body of Christ. After a brief rest period, and a very good time in Dallas, my arrival brought it all back again. Was I prepared to face this warfare again?

As I pondered on the matter, I arrived at the airport to find my friend Gordon Marshall who came to pick me up and take me home. Gordon parked his car on the roof of the airport. Well wouldn't you know it, we were stuck in the elevator at the airport for at least five to ten minutes. It was an old metal elevator filled with people. It seemed like we had been stuck in that elevator for a lifetime. Fear rose up again and I told Gordon about my problem. My stomach was weak and my heart started beating real fast. Sooner or later I would have broken out in a cold sweat and would not have been able to breathe. These symptoms are very real. I was in a panic. Gordon said, "Jesus is with us", and right at that moment, the doors opened. Isn't it just like God to quicken my spirit to write a book on fear?

A day or two after my arrival, I called my friend Pastor Gail who has a deliverance ministry in the inner city to tell her of my episode at the airport. I told her I thought the fear had left once I prayed it after my first ordeal two years ago at the office. She phoned a few days later and shared about her experience with anxiety. Her fear was so bad; she was at a restaurant and could not swallow food. She was so hungry. Her sister told her it was anxiety.

When she counseled me, she told me to ask God to take control of the situation if it ever rose up again. Say, "Lord, I cannot control this situation, take it from me." She said, "If the same situation presented itself in the future; and it happens again, just pray that prayer." I thank God for friends like Gordon and Gail who encourages my heart in sharing their experiences and recommending solutions.

Fear is not from God. (2 Tim. 1:7).

I have known people who were so fearful of being alone and rejected that they used no discretion at all in choosing who they would associate with, who they would sleep with, or who would control their lives. Cults and sects look for people who are very vulnerable to these characteristics.

Terrorists today use fear tactics by threatening the lives of people in many nations and they actually act upon many of them. Oral abuse can be very harmful to any individual. We must always be strong, courageous, prayerful, and steadfast knowing that God will prevail in every situation. Faith in God is the key in overcoming fear.

Our focus should be first on Jesus, then on others, and thirdly on ourselves. Once our priorities are in order, our lives will be. Jesus is no respecter of persons and we are never alone with Him in our lives. He is the answer to all our fears.

PASTOR'S COMMENTS

We have seen how the spirit of fear leads to destruction, affliction, deception, control, and occult activity all of which when allowed become strongholds in our lives. Fear can even cause you to come under bondage that will affect your physical condition as well.

Moses' success was largely due to continuously seeking God, knowing Him, and obeying His word. He pressed on in prayer for people who were complaining and grumbling and encouraged their hearts. He believed God for victory in battle and did not fear the outcome.

The spirit of fear is one of the greatest weapons in Satan's arsenal. Only our belief in the power of God and our willingness to seek Him in prayer can disarm him. The only way to combat fear and loose its hold is to seek God daily, receive His peace and presence, and live a life worthy of your calling and purpose. We are all leaders, but we must first let God take the lead. As we follow Jesus Christ, our Great Leader, we begin to fill our hearts with His word and carry it that we may pour it out to others. Jesus is our example. As we become more like Him and His divine nature, we extend our hand to touch people in our families, communities, co-workers, and the world.

Man was created for divine guidance. We become dissatisfied and restless when we don't surrender our lives to the Lord allowing Him to take control. Our constant unbelief and interference with God's plan and purpose for us bring about failure in getting to where we need to be. As a result, we lie in an empty dry place like the wilderness grumbling and complaining. Jesus invites the thirsty and the hungry to drink and eat at His table; to be satisfied at His feast. Are there people out there who have missed their leadership role in the kingdom of God. Seek Him out!

Man's defiance and rebellion makes it difficult for all leaders (secular or spiritual) to maintain peace and for God to bless and protect His people. The

Creator must maintain control and God cannot maintain control without our cooperation.

Our nation's leaders today are in jeopardy because people's rights have become more important than a leader's lawful right to rule. There is war, chaos, and every kind of disorder when God is not in control for He is a God of Order.

The word of God says we all fall short of God's glory; so let's grow up a little taller by leaving our childish ways and reaching up higher for a God Who is greater.

As a Leader, Moses never had a desire to become famous but only wanted to seek God and deliver His stubborn obstinate people. He braved the wilderness for decades and accomplished his task by listening to the voice of the Lord and following His commands. From centuries past, the name of Moses is renowned and widespread among the nations of the world. Movies have been filmed about God's call on his life and the study of the Exodus still rings true in the hearts of man to be free from the bondage of fear and sin.

"I will seek the Lord and He shall hear me to deliver me from all my fears." (Psm. 34:4).

This book was written through the instruction of the Holy Spirit of God to edify the Body of Christ.

www.ingramcontent.com/pod-product-compliance
Lightning Source LLC
LaVergne TN
LVHW051559080426
835510LV00020B/3057